THE ♡FFICIAL P♡ETS' GUIDE T♡ PEACE

Journal of Modern Poetry 18

Chicago Poetry Press, Chicago, Illinois
Copyright © March 2015 by CJ Laity
ChicagoPoetry.com | PoetryAward.org
Printed in the United States of America.

Cover Art by Itala Langmar
Illinois Landscape #1 Summer
10x20 Acrylic on Canvas
Collection of Dante Ferrario
earth sculptor. Plainfield, Illinois
www.evanescentart.com

Spread the Peace
Order copies of this book at
PeacePoetry.net

No part of this book may be reproduced or used in any form
or by any means without permission in writing from the publisher,
except for short excerpts used within the body of articles or reviews

YOUR GUIDES TO PEACE

Amanda Layman, 16

B Diehl, 38

Barbara Bridges Gylland, 17

Candace Armstrong, 11, 32

Candace Kubinec, 29

Carla Eisenberg, 77

Carolyn Clark, 14

Casey Derengowski, 76

Chris Reid, 69

CJ Laity, editor

David Nekimken, 47

Deborah Rohde, 10, 25

Deborah Nodler Rosen, 88

Donal Mahoney, 9, 26

Duane Christianson, 80

Ellen Savage, 44

Irfanulla Shariff, 28

Iris Orpi, 84

Itala Langmar, cover art, 48

Jennifer Kress, 62

JoAnne Blackwelder, 37

John J. Gordon, 42

Josef Venable, 64

Joseph Kuhn Carey, 41, 46

Joseph Glaser, 30

Kate Koten, 20, 58

Kathy Lundy Derengowski, 82

Laura Lee, 33

Linda Leedy Schneider, 27

Lynn Veach Sadler, 18

Mara Adamitz Scrupe, 65

Margaret Dubay Mikus, 56

Marian Kaplun Shapiro, 34, 55

Marilyn Peretti, 87

Mary Jo Balistreri, 43

Mary Langer Thompson, 60

S. M. Kozubek, 40

Nancy Heggem, 83

Peter Rodenby, 86

Richard King Perkins II, 66

Robin Lily Goldberg, 13

R.P.Muha, 21

Susan Beall Summers, 73

Susan Schaefer, 68

Tamara Tabel, 74

Thelma T. Reyna, 12

Tobin Fraley, 50

Tracie Padal, 31, 78

FIVE STEPS TO PEACE

1. Let the Light In
2. Be Enchanted
3. Enjoy an Interlude
4. Declare a Truce
5. Finish

STEP ONE

Let the Light In

Donal Mahoney

Saint Louis, MO

WHEN MY WIFE IS IN HER GARDEN

When my wife is in her garden,
she becomes a ballerina
moving with the morning breeze
through hollyhocks and roses,
peonies and phlox.
There is music only she can hear.
It's been that way for 30 years.
I never interrupt her dance

not even when the house caught fire
early in the morning. I didn't holler out
the way another husband might
if he had never had a gardener for a wife.
Instead I called the firemen,
and while they were on their way,
I poured water from the sink
on the growing conflagration.

My efforts proved to be in vain.
The firemen arrived too late and so
the house is now a shell of smoke.
The garden still looks beautiful
yet I have no idea what I'll say
when my wife comes back inside.
But if she's toting roses to arrange
she may not notice any change.

Deborah Rohde

Northbrook, IL

I WORRY ABOUT THE CHIPMUNKS

An abundance of chipmunks rule this season,
replacing the rabbits, those garden denizens,
eaters of fresh buds, destroyers of colored
harmony in my backyard picture-scape.

Gone are the long-eared, puff-tailed,
silent hoppers to unknown destinations,
perhaps on sabbatical for advanced
education or perhaps on extended vacation.

The new tenants race across the sidewalk
as if late for a critical appointment. They
seem flustered and anxious, looking for a lost
soul mate or for the next big idea.

With their stylish patterned coats of camouflage
the chipmunks are smaller and cuter than the bunnies,
but nevertheless engender concern for the hectic,
frantic minuets they turn below my shadow.

I worry about the psychological state
of these little rodents, want to cup
them in my hand, pet and give comfort.
Yet, I think I prefer the mellow hares.

Although voracious in their leveling,
the rabbits exude a polite demeanor,
an Eddie Haskell charm, and they are sedate,
always sober, monkish, peaceful, satisfied

Candace Armstrong

Murphysboro, IL

APRIL

My garden waits in soggy splendor,
full of secret promise beneath the soil.
It is nothing if not patient,
 waiting all these fallow months
  for the earth's return to warmth
   to be tickled again by my rake and hoe
    massaging away the crusty surface
     and caressing its timid offerings
      as they peek their tiny green heads
       into the wonder beyond the soil line
        the day after a storm.

Thelma T. Reyna

Pasadena, CA

LET THERE BE LIGHT

I flood my rooms each daybreak--
slide drapes, lift shades, swing doors to
do the god thing: bring in light.

Outside, the moon's a faded coin
on trees and clouds, an old woman with
her luster stripped who knows and waits.

Inside, the sink streaks gold, rays swathe
stone floors, the cat blinks and slinks down
from the tabletop, sun-blind.

My calendar can't tell me how my day
will go, lauded or denuded, how far my
psyche slides, or if I shine.

But at dawn, my hands are wands
that banish blackness, for it's true: what they
say, about god inside, god in each of us, how

we're
all
god.

Robin Lily Goldberg

River Forest, IL

SCENTS

As siblings in the sandbox

we can render Band-Aids unnecessary

by rotating Pinocchio's apostrophe's

and releasing cotton candy into the wind

YIN YANG

sweat seeps into styrofoam,

oozing over
from the neighbor's porch,

I worry
about metals and radicals,

but then I stretch the sun
and see
what is purely ours

DAYLIGHT SAVINGS

The Sun slides closer
    to the Moon
        in her mossy slippers
    for a frugal feast
    of buttered clouds,
        glass-blown gourds,
           and powdered pinecones

Carolyn Clark

Rockville, MD

CRESCENT TRAIL POEM

Running down the Crescent Trail
much warmer than I'd thought,
just before Dalecarlia tunnel
wind zipped off my cap,
my hand caught
a spinning pinnate
brazen yellow.
Images fused like bone
clapped together over and over,
the slap of vertebrae shrinking,
expanding - a runner's dreamscape.
Why do we run?
We are captured in a dream:
Today's trail riddled with leaves,
our fortunes unstrained
in a bottomless cup of tea.

On the way back I stop cold:
a new bench, its bright plaque

In memoriam Jane Sisco 2008
   Long may you run

boldly etched, tells me everything,
explains the unanswered calls.
The last time I saw you was at our gym,
you were bruised wholly green,
told not to run any more,
going in for a brain scan.
That was the last time we spoke
until now - this brazen new bench invoking
a shock of tears, silent, insistent:
rest and go on. Why do we run?
To keep balance in our lives, seek peace
in jagged constellations underfoot.

Jane, *I saw the most beautiful things on the trail today.*
Shall I tell you?
Two deer eating among the kudzu undetected,
and the runners I saw today,
even before your bench found me
this warm November afternoon,
seemed unusually friendly.

Amanda Layman

Joliet, IL

APRIL SONNET

Folding chairs poise in April's driveway
      Gutters collect twigs cornucopia-style
Neighboring vents exhale challah bread alleyways
      Petticoats chat on a bench down mossy mile

Steam curls corners of propaganda pasted against sodden poles
      A brick bakery scoops muffins in a foggy window display
Isabelle St. balances buttoned collars and shiny dress shoe soles
      Clicks of music fragments against an active marble stairway

Beckoning church bells precede a friendly hand grasp
      The clergyman greets at the height of his white sleeve
Stained windows birth colors through sun-punched glass
      White dresses flow fragile in the fleeting spring breeze

Taped up sandwiches flirt BBQ smoke swirls
      Potpourri of Kaiser rolls in an open-sign's whirl

Barbara Bridges Gylland

Vashon, WA

EASTER MORNING

This daybreak no buses squeal to a halt, no commuters race by.

There is only the high-pitched whistle of robins, punctuated by the buzz of a zipping hummingbird and the gentle beat of feet marking time on the pavement.

The rising sun bastes damp, green fields with a buttery light, the earth steams warm and golden like freshly baked bread.

Newly cut grass washed by the rain and kissed by the rising sun mingles with air scrubbed fresh by steady showers.

Morning sun seeps into the bones, its warm amber syrup a delicious comfort.

Two crows scavenge freshly mown grass seeking worms driven aloft by last night's unrelenting rain, pastoral dumpster-divers hungry for treasure.

A bushy tail waves flirtatiously before disappearing into branches ablaze with blossoms, too busy to chat this Easter morn' when there are other nuts to engage.

The earthy perfume of this breathtaking dawn is suffused with innocence, a freshly bathed infant, tender and clean, bursting with promise and unsullied by yesterday.

Turning in to a shady glen the light dims, but the promise of the day burns bright, rekindling the belief that anything is possible.

Sun, light, green, warmth, cleansing showers, and quietude collide, flinging open the day's arms in a welcoming embrace that says rebirth is imminent.

Lynn Veach Sadler

Pittsboro, NC

SHAKING HANDS WITH MOUNTAINS

On the flight inside Alaska,
when we can see,
the mountains are black,
dark gray, stark,
snow slammed hard upon them,
breaking them into jags and peaks.

But on the ground,
those protecting Valdez are
voluptuously green (to the tree line),
furred velvet,
run through with mid-June snow,
spring's hurling, curling, frothing water.

Every walk envelops you
in water's sound, the smell
of Cold-Clear-Fresh.
Water in the motel tap, I think,
must be sluiced
in from mountain flow, glacial floe.

Take it in now, I think,
for local, wiseacre wisdom
says two days of rain,
two of cloud,
two fair, and
one whatever-it-wants-to-be.
I find the misted best,
for the mountains decamp
and move upon you,
would step on your flying heels.

A pox upon my Achilles tendon!
I stop short,
turn,
extend my hand
to the mountains.
Surprised
(and pleased),
they take it.

Kate Koten

Hinsdale, IL

CONTENTMENT:

I felt it.
I felt it as wind tickled and teased
the tips of the tall grass, as
birds sang, and white wisps whisked by.
I felt it as the thick grass caught
my trusting fall—
it's gentle fingers leaning, curving slightly,
so slightly.

I could trust the grass to
catch my fall, like some trust God
to give them hope and inner peace.
The faithful have something to lean on,
something to catch them when they fall.
Now, I see, stretched before me like strong,
trusting friends, the field of   reaching grasses.
I gave myself to them,
into their arms

I fell.

R.P.Muña

Valparaiso, IN

"WAVES / PARADES"

Thwarting / slogging / down the street
Approaching prisms / parked between
A sunbelt / mural / gathering
Hanging in / great luminosity
The airy / culmination / kicks
With flickered lights / and booming wisps
It pulses out / from where we sit
It lassos the sun / and everything within

Colors / kaleidoscopes / collide
Radiant / rainbows / revive
Hiding / under / translucent trees
Embracing / plastic / for sheltering
We ignore the pillow pulp / of fluff
While hanging out / on edgy bluffs
We sing / our mother / together / one
Children / forever / our god / the sun

Aura's / waves / on parade
Observing drones / bee line the stage
We sought out / we trekked our way
Culmination / succumbed by praise
So I see you / as you see me
Draped in / brilliant simile
For I am we / as you are me
Here forever / galaxies

STEP TWO♡
Be Enchanted

Deborah Rohde

Northbrook, IL

ENCHANTMENT ON THE DES PLAINES RIVER TRAIL

The woods are dense here, crowding the trail
whose thick tree canopy barely allows a peak
at the sun through pockets in the leafy ceiling

Shadows play on the crushed gravel path
while a darting chipmunk flirts across my line,
a mirage messing with my mind

As I pedal around a mossy bend, the thicket
clears and I am face to face with a majestic head
wearing a crown of towering antlers

His two eyes gape back at mine, as surprised
as I by this sudden chance encounter
I swear he does a double take

Then our gaze holds steady, his wisdom
shining deep into my soul, filling me
with gratitude, respect, even love

He turns back into the brush, beckons me
to follow, wills me to abandon my bike
I am hypnotized, mesmerized, helpless to disobey

Together we weave through buckthorn and maple
to the river, where the stag laps at the fresh drink,
cooled by last evening's thunder storm

Later, as I pedal to the trail end, crossing the last
river bridge, I look back and glimpse him in a stand
of oak near the water's edge, peacefully watching me

Donal Mahoney

Saint Louis, MO

THE RUBY THROATS

Hummingbirds dance
iridescence afire

around the red feeder
hung in the cedar

a symphonic swirl
ruby throats glistening

sipping sweet nectar
sipping until

it's time to jet back
to thimble nests.

The tiniest beaks
are open and waiting.

Linda Leedy Schneider

Grand Rapids, MI

THE MONARCHS ARE IN THE MILKWEED

She runs through the geometry
of apple trees to the meadow
where Queen Anne rules,
proud of her purple difference,
daisies bend in the breeze, hold secrets in soft petals,
and matronly milkweed waits. Monarchs circle,
swirl in orange masses like flames on a hearth.
The girl drops her net, holster, black boots,
and floats around the milkweed with the butterflies.
Her arms flutter.
Finally she sits still as a Petoskey stone,
holding hexagonal memories of the ancient sea,
curls into herself, watches the harlequin dance,
breaks a thick leathery leaf, touches it to her lips.
A monarch lands on her hand tastes the milk. She
sees the spotted body, black legs ending in claws;
orange dust flies around the pumping wings.
She lies back on the soft grass, watches
the butterfly walk across her belly, then soar
to the highest apple tree.
She gathers Queen Anne's lace and daisies.
The empty net slung over her shoulder
bumps her bare legs
where orange dust clings like a memory.

Irfanulla Shariff

South Elgin, IL

THE VALLEY OF BUTTERFLIES

At the valley
Of butterflies
In Rhodes, Greece
I encountered
Nature's love affair
Feisty flowers
Rainbow colors
Flying gorgeously everywhere
Beyond anybody's reach
Fluttering here and there
Once the caterpillars
Magically turned into animated fairies
Gently hugging the trees
With their soft and fragile wings
Their inexplicable performance
Has fully mesmerized
Thousands of travelers
Enjoying the splendors
Of this world
And to be one of them
I am so gratified

Candace Kubinec

Greensburg, PA

SNOWBOUND

flake after flake

descend silently

flake after flake

clothe naked shrubs

and tree branches in

brilliant white robes

white on white flakes

drift silently landing

in cottony piles

settling into an overstuffed

leather chair I cover myself

with a plaid throw

pick up an unfinished book

a yellow cat jumps up on my

lap, purring, and I sigh

Joseph Glaser

Chicago, IL

PENELOPE

her tapestry is shrinking
threads dull and fraying

restored every day but less
scenes of daily life
eat   drink   pee   poop
faint purring
sleep sounds
gentle   soft
almost inaudible

wobbly rear legs
weave side to side
like Jayne Mansfield
with a walker

spring no more
lift me
hold me
pet me forever

heaven on a lap
distilled essence of cat
sweetness remains

meow...

Tracie Renee Amirante Padal

Palatine, IL

NOVEMBER

In the wind of my walk,
dry leaves scatter.
            I want to travel too—
                    that tender distance
                            between your arms
                                    and mine
                        opens wide.

                All night long,
            wishes gather like dew.

            Frost-jeweled grass
                stills its wave
under the light of hard stars.

It is morning,
but only just.

In the half-dark
of the waning moon,
your breath is slow
with dreaming.
The dog beats paws
against the rug
in other rooms,
running in his sleep.
Day creeps through the door-crack,
hangs in the air like the heat
of your breath. (In the bed,
I move closer to you, and whisper
Keep.)

Candace Armstrong

Murphysboro, IL

OBIT

The coarse short hairs and sharp nails
of the oblivious puppy scratch small
children in their romping play.
The soft old dog snores
at the feet of the reader.

Crumbs of buttered toast shower grease spots
across the cluttered breakfast table.
An opened newsprint page
records a sprinkling of the faces
of newly-appointed angels.

Laura Lee

Lombard, IL

OPEN

It's the spring wind
the open window
the shoots coming up.
It's sun gold on green:
I hear you once again
in the rustling drapes
smell you once again
in the rich brown earth
feel you once again
in the gentle breeze.

AFTER POETRY CLASS

slivered moon
seen between
Tribune Towers
stops traffic
chirping of crickets
continues under
the lines after
trains pass

Marian Kaplun Shapiro

Lexington, MA

BEFORE (THE) AFTER (QUAKER MEETING)

Quiet.

Door open. Bird sings.

Quiet.

Bird sings. Tree

sways. Breeze

bends branches.

Quiet.

You rise.

Consider the leaf,

you say, that's blown

through the door. Like

the spirit, free to come in.

You sit.

Quiet.

Quieter.

STEP THREE

♡

Enjoy an Interlude

JoAnne Blackwelder

Ocean City, NJ

TO A SURFER

The deep waves originate when two fluids, or gases (or sea and air), move past one another at different speeds. At the boundary, the interaction produces a sequence of crests that rise gently and then curl into chaotic turbulence.-- the **New York Times**, *April 20, 2010*

to a surfer news of a storm
coming up the coast
is occasion to call friends

and watch for high tide
when the dark mounds
will rear up and roll in

time to sense how feet
tingle and cling
to the board's shudder

time to at last to lift
on the wave
and learn to dance

to a surfer
too far out
is where to be

to be flipped into the deep
by a breaker is
to be almost right

to a surfer having feet
on a board heading
at the end of the world

is to ride ecstasy
in the moment before
it crashes into chaos

B Diehl

Phillipsburg, NJ

REINS

She pulls on her cowgirl boots
and heads for the mounting block across the field.

From out there, she must not see me;
she must not see the way my skin glows —
electrically vibrant, yet muddily green —
ugly. She must not see this.
And for that, I suppose I'm grateful.

My lady's purpose has lungs; it breathes.
And as she swings her right leg over the creature,
it seems to accept her intentions.
The beast obeys when she tugs at the reins —
and off they go, clouding the air with dust,
leaving behind the "what ifs" and the "whys."

Watching as she circles the arena,
it's all I can see: surreal, playwright-majestic —

an immortal glow that could only
be matched by the power of the sun —
a gleaming radiance, protruding from her pores —
mythical, hardly unlike the fire of a phoenix.

Now, abruptly, the muddy green of myself evolves,
blooming into the most delicate shade of purple.

She tugs at the reins, and I echo her now,
in the very same way teenagers mimic their idols.
She cannot see them, but I have my own reins here.
I tug and tug and tug, and my tangled thoughts
begin to unravel: out come the words — pouring, pouring.
On and on glows the yellow, the lavender....

It's all so bright now: these shades, this art!
Her yellow breathes life into the entire field —
and my lavender is gone, abducted by gold.

A collage of letters, the clopping of hooves,
splashes of color — and a clear mind is born.

Holly, I live to prevent your tears.
Thank you for the poem.

S. M. Kozubek

Chicago, IL

ON THE COURSE AT DAWN

No one but a groundskeeper
raking bunkers
and a red fox
trotting across the fairway,
its streaming tail
reflects the grapefruit sun.
Though off the tee my ball
grazes a trunk
bounds past trees--
and on the green
lines a trail through the dew,
glides,
then sputters
past the hole,
the morning air is crisp,
the day glistens
and the walk restores
in harmony with
this quiet,
more than decent life.

Joseph Kuhn Carey

Glencoe, IL

TWO-MAN CROSSCUT SAW

The two-man crosscut saw sliced through
the log with cool ripping efficiency but only
if you got the rhythm and angle right with your
pushing pulling partner on the other side,
sawdust flying and sweat dripping down foreheads
and arms, you work as one as well as you can
and progress jaggedly down through the wood
until the piece finally falls off and you pause and laugh
and look into each other's eyes and high five
since you beat the other log-cutting team
up on the widened dirt and stone path in the Black Forest woods
before you head over to the big thick log where you
can try to pound long dark nails with one stroke with the
narrow backside of an axe blade or hammer (which as it turns
out, is pretty tough to do and not many succeed), followed
by tossing a hammer end-over-end at balloons attached to a board
you get the hang of the toss after a few tries and explode
a few for fun and then watch your youngest son nail balloon
after balloon with amazing ease as if he's Buffalo Bill, Annie Oakley
& Calamity Jane rolled into one in a Wild West Show Shooting Contest
in a huge canvas tent somewhere out in the Dakotas, but then it's off to
a timbered house down the road with accordion music and song, good beer
and schnitzel and before you can say "Eins, Zwei, Drei, G'Suffa!", everyone is
up and dancing in the center of the room, with bright wide happy smiles
as if riding on the softest highest clouds around the world and seeing
all the tiny sights below, could there be any better moment
than this that sums up the fleeting essence of life, to laugh and love
and eat and drink with family around a carved wooden table surrounded
by thick timbers and gorgeous, rollicking, magical musical notes that
wind us all together like the sturdiest twine that rolls back in history
to the earliest fires and voices lifted loud above the crackling, warm
fire and cave-painting party din.

John J. Gordon

La Grange, IL

INTERLUDE

I intended to occupy this mid-evening
with pages of "Parrot & Oliver",
while snatching glances of gold,
crimson and purple hues promised
by the setting sun's rays dancing off
clouds suspended over Lake Michigan.
My favorite deck chair provided
the perfect perch.

During one transition from novel to clouds,
I spotted a neighbor easing by in his kayak.
His leisurely pace in shallow water,
indicated a short excursion.

I devoured another chapter as the clouds dressed
in deepening shades. He returned, settled
just offshore, facing the eastern horizon.
He sat back. The boat floated in place.

A squawking seagull briefly broke
the intense silence while warding off intruders
nearing its treasured stretch of beach,

I fixated on the man, kayak and surrounding water.
The stillness transformed my vista
into a stunning life-size watercolor,
the personification of serenity. I drifted
into a cerebral connection. My worries ebbed.
My mind flooded with buoyant images.
When my consciousness abruptly re-surfaced,
he was pulling the kayak out of the water.

The next morning as he packed, I offered
a simple, *safe journey home.*

Mary Jo Balistreri

Genesee Depot, WI

BOATING ON THE YERRES

Men lift the sky
in a shower of veiled hues, wooden paddles
dipping deep in the liquid silk of the Yerres.

With rippled strokes, they guide their skiffs,
slip silently between rows of poplars.
          A woman watches from the sanatorium, sees
trees shimmy in the skimmed wakes.

The green sheen of reeds begins to sweep her mind
          clean of all but the light, the men and the charmeuse
skein of river become shadows in the sun-drunk air.

Closing her eyes, she drinks the breeze, the stillness
          of this country afternoon, the lap of water on hull
as soothing as a lullaby.
          Shifts of color and luminosity flicker behind her eyelids.

In the cradle of her boat, she is alive to each vibration,
          braided into the melody of river music.

Ellen Savage

Highland Park, IL

IN THE COMPANY OF ANGELS

The diary opens to the page
   where she keeps it
      She likes to take it out
         brush its soft, delicate pink
           over her upper lip
              conjure the memory.
            It was a gift.
                 It is confirmation.

Muscle against headwind
   in search of the sand
      Paddle in gray chop
         Pray that it won't rain
         Far across the bay
            Around Inner Key
              Aim for the channel
              Finally still water

No beach is in sight
   Pine scent on each side
      leads to a dead end
         untamed and deserted
           except for a presence
              in the trees on the left
                 Branches sway under
                   meaningful weight.

Enter the cul-de-sac
  of their private world
    tree limbs bow as six rise
      rose petal pink
        bent wings like angels,
          prehistoric heads incongruous,
            long-handled spoons protruding,
              inspire as they circle, a living halo.

 She dreams of going ashore
   to become one of the pines, her toes
     curl in the mud, her knees
       hover at the water's surface
         her arms outstretched,
           never tire, ready to receive
             one of nature's seraphim.

She meditates how mystical
  life is when feeling lost
    on her way, she blunders
      upon a blessing so unexpected
        she experiences a lightness.
          What else could it mean but
            a small piece of her has died,
              preceded her to heaven?

She glances down—she floats
  on a mirror of clouds
    and there the gift: a single feather.
      She scoops it from the water, hoards it
        like a miser, a palpable trace
          of the day that she lingered
            in the company of angels.

Joseph Kuhn Carey

Glencoe, IL

IN THE OPEN CABLE CAR

In the open cable car swinging gently
up above the endless vineyard rows
shooting out in all directions
like an amazing crazy quilt
just beyond the town of Rudesheim,
after a drizzly but scenic Rhein river
boat ride from easy-going Wiesbaden
(with bright sunshine and strong
surprise winds on deck on the last
river bend around the castle-strewn
side hills, whipping coats, pants
and hats like flags in a micro-burst),
there's a soft quietude that plays like a
beautiful, lulling symphony, almost
as if the Lorelei is singing to sailors
and trying to make them crash onto hidden
Rhein rocks, but here you're hanging
in space in a tiny metal car, alone with
your thoughts, hopes and dreams,
with no windows and the sky your
only neighbor, a meditation on
everything and nothing at the same time,
the river glinting, the ships moving slowly
like sugar cubes in molasses, the whole
world one big kaleidoscope of color,
the wind picks up and rocks the car a bit
and with white-knuckle happiness
you glide the rest of the way up to
the top of the hill looming tall over
the picturesque, oompah-band sized town.

David Nekimken

Chicago, IL

PEACE DAY 2 0 1 1

The flags hung in the air
As colorful bits of confetti
In silence
Fluttering to the haunting tones
Of a Native American flute
Harkening back to
The ancient ways
The ancient wisdom,
Then moving slowly and proudly
One by one
All 193 recognized members of the human family
Into the spotlight
To the thunderous and compassionate
Wishes for peace within its borders---

And a peace wish to recognize
The unrecognized peoples of the world,
Our stepsons and stepdaughters,
As politicians' opposition
Rears up like a frightened horse---

Then a climactic call for
Peace in the world,
For a long moment
We understood
All the colors of Oneness
All the sounds of Oneness,
No separate flags
No lines of separation,
We are One...

Every day
Every hour.

Itala Langmar

Kenilworth, IL

QUASI UNA FANTASIA
Almost a Fantasy

The painter's work,
pale abstractions of
non-Euclidian geometry,
hang bathed in light,
entities self-invited
like distant relatives
consolidated against
the fading of youth.

She said: I wanted people
to forget about food
about cost of living,
aging, the visceral
ingratitude of kids.
I wanted to rescue them
from unnerving banality,
the obsession of shopping,
the terror of death.

I do what I do disregarding
the stock market, the art stars
their trends and dictates.
I do what I do by building
erasing caressing . . .
My works are my lovers
I keep them tied to my jeans
until they can stand
hermetic and graceful
all by themselves.

I make no plans in advance
consult no avatars,
the clouds, only the clouds
let me know when I am done,
when a piece has become
Quasi una fantasia.

Tobin Fraley

Mundelein, IL

CENTRAL PARK, 1993

One cloudless evening
when the tranquil twilight warmth
of early summer
brushes against you
and the air glows city-light orange,
untold thousands stroll,
same direction, no rush.

Some with folding chairs
beneath their arms.
Others carry baskets,
blankets and bottles.
The solemnity broken only by
quiet conversations trickling
through the crowd.

We all ease
down the sidewalk
past buildings that seem
as if they had stood for centuries.
Walking in reverence
as pilgrims who have come
to be lifted and caressed.

And we are not disappointed.
Places are found,
blankets unfurl,
wine opens,
Zabars treats consumed.
Soon murmurs, followed by thunder
of a million clapping hands.

Then silence.

Slowly the sound unfurls.
Luciano's exquisite voice coats us
with a rain of notes.
I lie back, feel the soft grass
brush against my fingers
as the music washes away
whatever is left of the world.

Time stops
until, too soon,
with Nessun dorma
the magic ends,
leaving
us all
breathless.

STEP FOUR
Call a Truce

Marian Kaplun Shapiro

Lexington, MA

VOWS

                                      If
lovesongs grew fragrant blossoms, flowers
       would find ways to rhyme. Bells would bloom
in gardens of *as long as we both shall live*.
       Gracenotes of *I do*'s would intermarry
in lavaliers of trills. The aisles would be strewn
       with cadenzas, the altars painted brilliant
with brushes of light (*moon/sun/stars)*
       Haikus of hope would spray the evening sky
with roman candles. Sugared strawberries
       would serve as semi-colons. Sweet wine
would curve us into hollyhocks.

                                        If
we were red red roses we would row
row row our boats gently down the stream.

Margaret Dubay Mikus

Lake Forest, IL

WATCHING BOATS ON THE LAKE
Navy Pier, Chicago

With lips unused to kissing
kisses sought and won
and won again
better this time.

Remembering kissing
as part of everyday living
coming, going, being together
reluctantly pulled apart.

Memorable kisses that drew breath
from your lungs to mine, that lasted forever
or almost, but not quite
kisses that bandaged or bonded

not like super glue, but like braided silk
threads, deceptively strong together
though apparently fragile, soft and thin.
Nothing could prematurely part them.

Lips longing to be asked
afraid of disappointment
or afraid of nothing after all this
still open with promise.

In the course of things, both before and after
speed boats, sailboats, police boats, cruise ships,
fireboats, skiffs, sloops, dinghies, jet skis, tugboats, pirate boats
and one four-masted, gaff-rigged schooner.

Sun sets in the west as expected
behind the striking city skyline silhouette.
Left over sun plays on ripples
as the golden slant slowly turns dark.

Mosquitoes buzz
gulls swoop
air is still and clear,
we could see the smoke stacks

all the way from Calumet Harbor.
Nowhere to go, but here
a witness to life unfolding
no rush. To remember life could be like this.

Kate Koteñ

Hinsdale, IL

FOR ANSLEY

You are leaving,
headed into that deep bowl
of independence.
Your future—heavy, steep
sits there
waiting to be full.
You will pour yourself into it
like you do with friendships.

Remember Herman Melville,
he introduced us.
You returned from France
vibrant like the stained glass of Notre Dame,
confidence splashing under eyes and cheeks,
a seed planted.

Remember that night,
we discussed our future weddings,
equally agreeing they are long to come.
"You will be my maid of honor," I said.
Your eyes—a crescent moon swiftly filling, as they do
when your smile adorns your face,
more genuine than any Peruvian Lily.

Remember Thanksgiving,
bellies warm and bulbous with
Amarula, Eggnog, Baileys, and Pumpkin Beer.
The sweet taste of cloves lingering on lips and tongue,
smoke from the cigarettes hugging,
pipe tobacco tucking us into
folds of sand.

You filled notes and music in my mailbox,
made steaming cups of hot chocolate
warm with hope
as men sifted through our lives.
You embraced me with arms of roots,
ceaselessly nourishing.

Mary Langer Thompson

Apple Valley, CA

WAVING MAN OF BERKELEY
For Joseph Charles

He didn't travel far,
simply to the curb in front of his home
to wave at us
for thirty years every morning
tell us to
keep smiling.

He waved to
the business executive
the homeless
the teacher
the student
the hooker
the reformer
to wish us well
until the strength in his arm
began to wane and
he gave his final
gesture of grace.

Now the mourners
pass by his casket
and follow his lead.
I feel my own arm
complete its arc,
become a salute.

It will be hard to keep smiling, Joe,
now that God's granted you
a waiver on waving.

Mary Langer Thompson

Apple Valley, CA

TRUCES

I carry the hot ham to this table.
Ring the dinner bell.
People lag in chairs, on couches,
choose cherries covered
with chocolate and gooey gossip.
One snaps her camera
while the meal grows cold.

1914, in No Man's Land
on the Western Front,
Germans softly sang
Silent Night.
Soon men emerged from trenches
to exchange greetings,
play soccer,
give proper burials.

One descendant says,
It's a place everyone should come to.

Jennifer Kress

Wood Dale, IL

TENDER

His fingertips trailed lazily, charting
his favourite course, the gentle
wake-up call of sunrise. a heavy fall
of the ink spilled sky, absent of
golden starshine as each twinkle
fades to grey

Blush and orange blossoms bloom
among the rosey crush he follows in
the wake of tender kisses; feathered
brow to the embouchure from which
spills her sighs of enchantment

He gently pleads with her "rise my
love, come away; make haste as I
hear tender melodies rising within
me"...

As he moves over the sunswept
horizon of her, the sounding of the
bell's toll unfolding the dawn, as
much as petals falling soft and free
to light

Garden of worship revealed, her veil
drawn back to fragrant fields of
tender beauty; she offers to him the
bounty of her sweetest nectar

Nursed from her honeysuckle lips,
fresh nourishment spills and tips her
dew-lashed eyes as he drinks from
the pooling depths of her love

He breathes harmony over her star-
dusted skin, teasing new found life
into sleep weary limbs; unfurling as
the winter flocks take flight

Rising to meet the joy he brings,
discarding all scent of nightshade
burden; the miracle of their dawning
fire is birthed in the new light of day,
renewed.

Josef Venable

Harwood Heights, IL

FINDING EMPATHY ON A FRIDAY

Sitting across from you
on a lumpy, cream-colored couch,
your cat prowling across the top frame,
and one lonely bottle of sweet red
resting emptily on the coffee table,
while yours chills in the fridge,
half finished.
I'm finally speaking of what's on my mind
a year and a half after
we met.

Sitting across from you
on a lumpy, cream colored, couch
in a second floor apartment living room
that feels now
like a mountain monastery hearth
away from it all, high up in the clouds,
and out of the cold.

I am saying things to you now,
a year and a half after
we met,
I've trouble confessing to a poem
which cannot breath or answer back
or shed a tear for me.

Sitting across from you,
my mind and soul let down
from the cross I hung them on,
like towels wet with spilled wine,
I can be honest with myself
through you
staring back at me
through glazed blue eyes.

Mara Adamitz Scrupe

Philadelphia, PA

NOW

I only know you as you are now and if I stand naked examining pressing

lumps, assessing my ass in the mirror, what you see: old body liver

spots,

>   wrinkles arrayed in patterns

round my eyes,   aged flesh, you know me as only I am now,   past
time

and if I fall your crooked hands fingers catch me fixed in my sight,

>   make a net,
>   right me

A woman decides this is enough,   enough,   and she is through and there
will never

>   ever be   more than this,   in this life.

Richard King Perkins II

Crystal Lake, IL

DISTILLERY OF THE SUN

I.

She's a complicated person; one of those rare people
who laughs only because she's had a tough life
and can't see it at all.

What she can see, with eyes audacious and ever-reaching,
is your inner-landscape releasing oxygen

that settles upon nightfall and nearby skies
celebrating at the top of your mind and eyebrow.

It's complex, what she does; beyond the deepest blue,
evoking, in her down-to-earth way, an invitation:

Come; there is so much more laughter to be revealed
and into your subtle hands will settle the essential droplets
of form and identity.

II.

She asks where everyone has gone to
while plucking at greenery,
picking berries in purple and red,

but thinking not of an alcohol made from fruit or honey
but a drink made from grain

and that we are all just spirits absently floating
out of and into the distillery of the sun

near-perfect impurities
taken by an isolation of breeze

that touches our forehead,
soon to be memory; consumed, forgotten,
perhaps never noticed at all.

Susan Schaefer

Chicago, IL

A WOMAN MUST KNOW

The smallest fish in the depths of the ocean.
Pushed to and fro by swelling waves' motion.
Fins and tail swaying, jaw and gills closing.
Opening, closing. Opening, closing.

The swings of a marriage, long and yet struggling.
Beginning and ending. Beginning and ending.
When jaws are closed tightly, breathing is hard.
The marriage is over. Dead because marred.

The marriage is over. Regretting the past.
Once she believed the marriage would last.
Regretting, regretting, she needs to have courage.
To live in the now, the past is submerged.

A fish doesn't try to swim with control.
A woman must know, it's time to let go.
Time to let go. Time to let go.
A woman must know it's time to let go.

chris reid

Chicago, IL

GAMES FOR GIRLS

It's time, maybe well past time,
For new action figure
A peacekeeping heroine
Made of bendable plastic parts

We'll give her a laudable super skill
Forget spider webs or x-ray vision
She will have an ability
Fitted to the modern millennium

What she'll have is the power
To stop an explosion
Just imagine the impact of
Her presence on this world at war

With a wave of her hand
A grenade would become a dud
After her knowing nod
No bomb could detonate

Her touch would extinguish
The fire in any firing pin
And landmines, being inert junk,
Could sit by the curb for recycling

(Dream House & accessories sold separately)

STEP FIVE

♡

Finish

Susan Beall Summers

Hutto, TX

PEACE ON YOUR PILLOW

At the end of a day
if your loved ones are safe, fed and happy
if you have accomplished something meaningful,
learned something new,
and shown someone you care,
you can lie down,
feel gratitude for all you have,
know it is enough.
As you drift toward sleep,
let bliss
envelop you.

You have found peace on your pillow.

Tamara Tabel

Barrington, IL

FALL BACK

Bedroom curtains flutter.
It's insistent, this fall wind,
peeking, closing, peeking,
like a child's game.

Kitchen dishes clatter,
my husband growls to clear
his morning throat,
my sons' man-boy steps
pound down the stairs.

Maggie paws at me,
beacon eyes burn
willing me to rise
asking Out? Now? Out?

I roll over, cover my head,
the bed deliciously warm
covers delightfully heavy
eyelids drifting shut.

I should treasure
this stolen hour, taken
back from spring, pen
a poem, coin a chapter,

or marvel at the marbled
clouds, filling my lungs
with the crisp autumn air,
the crunch of leaves
beneath my feet, invite

my husband back to bed, steal
kisses beneath the sheets,
rediscover our bodies, ourselves,
after a week as strangers.

But when I awake again
it is late, the sun strong,
the time already flown —
petals on the wind.

Casey Derengowski

San Marcos, CA

QUEST FOR PEACE AND QUIET

I'm the parent of three, two tomboys and an acrobat
I have an eighteen year contract with them (and then some)
I've acquired the ability to listen to three stereos simultaneously
the kids play rap, rock and hip-hop.

Would that I could hear but a single note of classical music.
I'm not one to complain, unless someone will listen
My requests are few and very simple-
I long for peace and might kill for quiet.

Who would believe this small house could hold so much chaos
there's the unremitting cacophony of dinner plates
which are handled more like sounding brass and tinkling symbols
while forks and knives challenge timpani for noise.

My ears are numbed by 200 decibels of the vacuum cleaner
my daughters take lessons on the horn and kazoo
big brother hammers away at the kettle drums
up the drive come friends with their 300hp muscle car.

Is there no P&Q between the womb and the tomb?
Being at my wits end, I took to the yard
seeking a cloister with silence and solitude-
it's the kids' cramped but distant tree house.

With book in hand-"Quiet on the Wester Front"
I nestled in the corner on a tattered quilt
When out of the rafters erupted two complaining doves
along with a family of squirrels from a cache of acorns.

This is all the result of Original Sin
It goes way back to Adam and Eve
I can't hear myself think with all this noise-
the school marching band is now passing by.

Carla Eisenberg

Hanover Park, IL

AWAKENING

Growing up, my mother and sister were morning people.
My father and I came alive at night. He and I agreed
morning conversation was unnecessary. A nod
or a wave worked just fine.

My mother and sister dove into the day
with a splash and climbed out at nightfall.
My father and I began by wading
into the shallow end and then slowly moved
into depth. Sometimes we got in over our heads.

At forty, my parents long gone,
I became a diver, arising with a full dose
of energy to greet the sun.
Friends who knew not to call in the morning
learned not to call in the evening.

As if a dormant fault line
had turned active, my world shook.
Whatever didn't shatter ended up
in a different place. Happiness,
though elusive, was suddenly clear.

Tracie Renee Amirante Padal

Palatine, IL

TRANSPOSITION OF GREAT PEACE AND WORRY

In the lingering moonlight of 4 a.m.,
my son's shriek shatters all hope of sleep.
Red-faced with wanting, pink-cheeked with passion,
he kicks, shakes, rattles the bars of his crib
and refuses to be still, refuses to fade quietly with the moon—

and you wouldn't think
this is a poem about gratitude and peace and joy—
            but it is.

My son was born quiet,
        the vessels in his heart backwards, pumping only
        stale, oxygen-starved air through his limbs, and
there in the delivery room, he curled into me:
        pale and limp,
        with heavy-lidded eyes blinking shut
        before they could even open,
        his small body vanishing
        into a complex web of wires and lines and tubes
        before he could even learn my touch.

I watched as he did not cry.
I watched as he did not move.
I watched surgeons track his pulse.
I watched machines breathe for him.
I watched my fingers worry tissue to dust.
I watched the seasons change through the slats in the hospital blinds:
        May Day mud   and fleeting green,
       a fury of color blanched to the wan monotony
       of snowandcold and sunandmoon, sun and

           the lingering moonlight of now.
                                   I am tired; he is not.
           He is not asleep. He is not quiet. He is not still.
           And you wouldn't think
           this is a poem about gratitude and peace and joy—
               but it is.
               The long scar on his chest trembles:
               brave and fierce and lovely alive
               with his breath—

       and I watch him:
               each heave of lung
                     a promise;
               each heartbeat
                   a fist.

Duane R. Christianson

Davidson, NC

YOU CAN DO ANYTHING YOU WANT NOW

You can do anything you want now:
paint the kitchen yellow,
the color that she hated,
forget her decades-long
commitment to sky blue.

You can stay out each night
until someone, Bengston, maybe,
the barman bachelor
who lives above an old maid's place,
turns lights out at the club.

You can empty out the fridge of beer
and return to aqua vitae and schnapps,
the stuff you used to knock back
with the boys you never spoke about
when you and they
got dressed up on Saturdays in Småland
and were ritually unaware
of where and who you were.

You can start playing
once more for cash at Euchre
instead of candy.
You can stop working
at Republic Furniture.
You can sell up.

And just now,
you can say anything at all.

The young clerk at the discharge desk
is not wise enough
to stop repeating policy
at what we all called Swede's.
You could tell her
she can damn well
wait for money.
But you will not.
You'll say instead,
"Send me the bill.
I did not expect
to walk out of here alone."

You don't know yet
that for a couple years
you'll choose to walk
into the whine of shop saws
to bring your lathe to life.
Your heart will never let you
give up making things.

You don't know yet
that you will paint the upstairs green
with the trim in pink,
that you will leave the kitchen blue
or that you will
keep her flower garden bright.

But most of all
you don't know yet
that for years
you will bring the gift of quiet
as if you had shaped it specially
for each one of us
and place it gently
in our hands.

Kathy Lundy Derengowski

San Marcos, CA

JUST ANOTHER ORDINARY DAY

Sometimes the day wraps itself around you, snug and warm.
This is the ordinary day, no crisis or anxiety.

You might beg to have a lifetime of these days

First, forego all risk, no racing or chasing, skiing or sky-diving.
Bypass love, too; no heart to be broken, no children to fret over
    No jealousy or grieving.
Close your eyes and ears to the pains of reality, the poverty, the wars,
    The ignorance and disease.

Impossible, this bargain we cannot strike
Not really living at all
Yet occasionally we are granted the blessing of an ordinary day.

Nancy Heggem

Palatine, IL

CHURCH BASEMENTS

Alone at the top of an 8000 foot ski run, I saw
the peaks and valley vast, the blue sky near and clear.
It must have been transformed by the breath of God.

I have stood in a circle of red rocks with the ashes
of my father, surrounded by his children and grandchildren,
aware of our ancestors, held in the hands of the Great Spirit.

But I have never been closer to God and Peace,
than in the basements of churches.

At an Assembly of God church in Wisconsin, where the print apron
clad women set the tables, gather the children, feed the men,
light 90 candles and lead the singing at my cousin's birthday.

In a suburban Catholic church, where ancient bean bag chairs circle
a teen age girl sitting on a sagging sofa, who is able to speak of her
father's cancer, surrounded by the caring, loving kids lounging there.

From the kitchen at the Lutheran church comes the sweet smell of
onions and meat loaf, apple pie and cornbread, warm in this
homeless shelter, tonight people will eat, talk and sleep safely.

Where the coffee is hot, folding chairs are set up, the friends of Bill W.
are ready in the basement of the United Methodist church and
"come to believe a power greater than self can restore them to sanity".

Iris Orpi

Lansing, IL

SKINNY DIPPING IN CASSIOPEIA

I let down my hair
for the wind to play with.
I tell myself
I'll untangle the strands
later, after the words have
been laid down on paper,
because my muse
will not be bothered
by scrunchies or watches
or tinted sunglasses.

I want to live within
a certain nudity
of sensibility,
like a closed wound
that's been through all
stages of healing;
the only thing left to do
is be allowed to breathe
and not be swathed
in layers of the nonessential.

I like to fall
asleep while dreaming
under the eaves of
quiet contentment
on idle afternoons with
only the breeze as lullaby,
and awaken to the gentle
caresses of the sun.

I like to have little birds
take refuge in
my hand-painted serenity,
the flapping of little bird wings
replaced by the patter of
little bird feet,
curious and carefree,
and believe in my heart
that the great and
powerful destiny
that directs my path
with certainty
has also set aside some
blank pages for me
to write on as I please.

Peter Rodenby

United Kingdom

THERE WAS A KIND OF PEACE IN THAT MOMENT

We missed the tide
the first wave break over the road

the causeway was beginning to flood
we had to turn back.

 hard as it was
we had made the only decision possible
but it was still sad
to be forced to leave the island.

On the mainland
from the shelter of the car
We watched
 as the tide raced.
 Ate lunch of oat cakes and cheese
while we talked and laughed
crushed in the back seat

And I knew
by your lips on my face
by the touch and feel of your passion
by the way your body responded to mine
that you were there for me
there was a kind of peace in that moment.

Marilyn Peretti

Glen Ellyn, IL

IF YOU HAVE YOUR HEALTH

you have everything, maybe,
but then the dog runs off,
you lose your 15-year job
with all the medical benefits,
and your son drops out of college
just when he's about to graduate.

In a park breathe in the cool air
on the finest of summer days,
fill your big bubble lungs
with nature's sweet fuel
for you have rocky days ahead.
Lean on the trees, the hardy giants
of this park, the statuesque oaks.

Keep this little oasis inside,
falling back on its nonchalance,
its grace and endurance,
even the tiny lake, its gray geese
poking at the picnic crumbs on shore.

Then go buy yourself roses
at Trader Joe's, stock up on dark
chocolate bars, and eat bowls
of coconut ice cream in the shade.

Deborah Nodler Rosen

Glencoe, IL

TO FINISH

Finished for me is the finest word.
Choices, decisions, mistakes made and done.
Something has been boundaried. I can hold
a piece of time that will not fade.
My puny mind that cannot tolerate
a moment's chaos within a larger plan,
longs to immobilize, to fence and gate—
petrify process and call it peace at last.
But if from the flowering crab apple tree
no petal ever fell, no footprint marred
the sand or snow, would I savor pure ecstasy,
orgiastic apogee, find strength to guard
the perfect sound and smell? Or would I long
for the grace of a child's unpracticed song?

MORE ABOUT YOUR GUIDES TO PEACE

Amanda Layman is a senior at Columbia College Chicago majoring in advertising with a focus in copywriting. Amanda says: "Whether it's advertising or poetry, words are my warmth—my favorite interpretation of humanity and nature."

B. Diehl is a 24 year old poet from Phillipsburg, New Jersey. He is currently working on his first collection of poems, *Zeller's Alley*, a book that he aims to have published by the end of 2016. More of his work can be found at Facebook.com/B.DiehlPoetry.

Barbara Bridges Gylland lives on Vashon Island in the state of Washington with her husband and two sons. When not writing she enjoys gardening, museum-going, helping colleges and universities with technology projects, the beauty of the Pacific Northwest and delighting in the company of friends and family

Candace Armstrong's poetry has placed in Dream Quest One and Illinois State Poetry Society contests and her work has been published in *The Lyric, MUSE, Distilled Lives Volume 2, Negative Suck* and on the ISPS website. She currently makes her home in the beautiful woodlands of Southern Illinois.

Candace Kubinec lives in Greensburg, Pennsylvania and is a member of the Ligonier Valley Writers. Her poems and short stories have appeared in *The Loyalhanna Review, Highland Park Poetry Muses' Gallery* and *Kind over Matter*. She is a finalist in the Highland Park 2015 *Poetry That Moves* competition.

Carla Eisenberg is the author of the poetry chapbook *A Moment Changes Everything*. Her poems have been published in the *Northwest Cultural Council Poet and Artist Chapbook* and in *JOMP 15*. She was a finalist in the 2004 Guild Complex Gwendolyn Brooks Open Mic. Awards.

Carolyn Clark, (Rockville, Maryland and Ithaca, NY) works variably as a teacher, writer-editor, and personal trainer. She first studied poetry under Archie Ammons at Cornell and continued on to study Classics and got her M.A. from Brown and Ph.D. from JHU. Her passions include riding, writing woodlands lyric poetry, and finding mythology everywhere - as can be seen in her first chapbook *Mnemosyne: The Long Traverse* (Finishing LIne Press, 2013).

Casey Derengowski honed his writing skills as a probation officer and, in retirement, is an active member of the Lake San Marcos Writers' Group.

Chris L. Reid, world traveler and ESL instructor, is a long-time Chicago area slam poet and past Contemporary American Poetry Prize recipient. Chris is a student of Arabic Studies at the University of Chicago and is a graduate of the University of Illinois.

CJ Laity is the publisher and editor of Chicago Poetry Press through which he has published over twenty anthologies of poetry. He is the author of several poetry books as well as three published fiction titles. He has been active as a poetry promoter in Chicago for going on thirty years.

David Nekimken is a senior citizen living in Qumbya Housing Cooperative in Hyde Park, Chicago. He is a graduate of Antioch College in Ohio and a former member of the Neighborhood Writers Alliance. He says: "The topic of peace in this issue of the Journal of Modern Poetry is a perfect fit. I am a cause for creating more peace in the world."

Deborah Rohde is a semi-retired healthcare construction executive who now teaches part time. Her poetry has appeared in *Distilled Lives, Your Daily Poem* and the *Muse's Gallery of Highland Park Poetry.*

Deborah Nodler Rosen is the author of several books including *sight/seer*, a collection of her travel poems, and *ANWAR EL SADAT*, a biography of the Egyptian leader. In addition she has edited the book *Where We Find Ourselves: Jewish Women Around the World Write about Home*. Rosen is an editor of *RHINO*, an award-winning poetry journal, and teaches poetry workshops in the school.

Donal Mahoney, a native of Chicago, lives in St. Louis, Missouri. He has worked as an editor for *The Chicago Sun-Times*, Loyola University Press in Chicago and at Washington University in St. Louis. He has had fiction and poetry published in *The Wisconsin Review, The Kansas Quarterly, The South Carolina Review, The Christian Science Monitor, The Beloit Poetry Journal, Commonweal, The Galway Review* (Ireland), *The Osprey Journal* (Wales), *Public Republic* (Bulgaria), and *The Istanbul Literary Review* (Turkey).

Duane Christianson has a BA in English from Principia College and completed all work for the doctorate except for the dissertation in English from University of Illinois, Urbana. He spent the last thirty years of his career in blind rehabilitation, the final twenty working for the Veterans Administration teaching blind veterans to use computers. His poem "You Can Do Anything You Want Now" was previously published in his book *Burning on the Mesa.*

Ellen Savage is a nurse, musician and nature lover who got serious about writing poetry after her yoga teacher introduced her to many wonderful poets and she found herself with time on her hands when her son left for college. Her book of poetry *Forever Linked* is forthcoming from Finishing Line Press.

Irfanulla Shariff has a great passion for writing inspirational poetry. His poems appeared in *The Sound of Poetry*, an audio collection. He was presented an International Poet of Merit Award by the International Society of Poets in 2002. He is a member of Illinois State Poetry Society and is a Computer Scientist and Telecommunications Engineer.

Iris Orpi is a Filipina writer living in Lansing, Illinois. She is the author of the novel *The Espresso Effect* (2010) and two books of compiled poems *Beautiful Fever* (2012) and *Cognac for the Soul* (2012). Her poems and essays have appeared in over a dozen publications in Asia, the United States and the United Kingdom.

Itala Langmar is an Illinois artist and has been painting and writing poetry since she was a girl in Venice, Italy. After gaining proficiency in English, she began writing poetry in English as well as Italian. Itala often informs her paintings with the text of her poems because choosing the right words and the perfect colors for them are mutually creative.

Jennifer Kress f/k/a Diane Anjoue lives in Wood Dale, Illinois where she has found the necessary peace to write poetry, prose and short stories for the last twelve years. She is humbled to have had a good number of her poems published by Chicago Poetry Press as well as by other great publications. The poem "Tender" was written as a poetic interpretive of the original piano composition written and performed by JDugger of hiskeystohernotes.tumblr.com. Visit Jennifer's blog at aclassofasin.tumblr.com.

JoAnne Blackwelder has published poems in *The Lyric, Poet's Review, The East Hampton Newsletter, Printing News* and in the anthology *Love Notes* (Vagabondage Press). She was a runner up in The Formalist (aka, Measure) sonnet contest of 1995. She will be a featured poet at the Beach Bards reading in Sea Isle City this coming September.

John J. Gordon is married and has three children and eight grandchildren. He is a member and former officer of the Illinois State Poetry Society and Poets & Patrons and has been published in *JOMP 15, 16*, and *17* as well as in *Prairie Light Review, Beaver Island Reader* and on several internet sites.

Josef Venable is the former Editor-in-Chief of Wilbur Wright College's literary magazine *The Wright Side*. He is an avid poet and student of history, a Civil War reenactor, a suburbanite wordsmith and a prospective educator of English and History.

Joseph Kuhn Carey's poetry book *Postcards from Poland* was selected as the third *Journal of Modern Poetry* Book Award winner and was published by Chicago Poetry Press in 2014. He is the recipient of an American Society of Composers, Authors and Publishers (ASCAP) / Deems Taylor award for music-related writing. His poem "In The Open Cable Car" was previously published on the Highland Park Poetry website in 2013. His book is available at PostcardsfromPoland.com.

Joseph ("Joe") Glaser spent most of his career in technology, but, in retirement, he pursued Liberal Arts and began writing poetry in 2008. His poems have appeared in print in *The Journal* (Northwestern University OLLI program), *Journal of Modern Poetry* through which he won the JOMP 16 Best Modern Poem Prize, and in *Distilled Lives Vol 2* (Illinois State Poetry Society). Joe also pursues candid travel photography and his photos have been published in the same media as his poetry.

Kate Koten enjoys reading and writing poetry when she isn't busy designing and making new jewelry and accessories for her Etsy and eBay stores. She acquires inspiration from the beauty and ugliness of the natural world, her memory and discovering new insights into her past and, most importantly—her friends and family. Her poems "Contentment" and "For Ansley" were previously published in *Camas*.

Kathy Derengowski is a Southern California poet active in the poetry community of North San Diego County. She has been a finalist in the San Diego Book Awards poetry chapbook category, and is currently co-submissions editor for *Summation*, the anthology from the poets and artists of the Escondido Municipal Gallery.

Laura Lee is the pen name of a Chicago area teacher and writer who has had her works published in the United Kingdom, Greece and the United States.

Linda Leedy Schneider, winner in the 2012 Contemporary American Poetry Prize, is a political activist, poetry and writing mentor and psychotherapist in private practice. She founded The Manhattan Writing Workshop and conducts workshops for The International Women's Writing Guild. Linda has written six collections of poetry including *Some Days: Poetry of a Psychotherapist* (Plain View Press) and edited two collections of poetry written by poets whom she has mentored: *Mentor's Bouquet* (Finishing Line Press) and *Poems From 84th Street* (Pudding House Publications). Her poem "The Monarch Are in the Milkweed" was previously published in *The Ambassador Poetry Project*.

Dr. Lynn Veach Sadler is a former college president who has published, in academics, five books and seventy-two articles. She has edited twenty-two books / proceedings and three national journals as well as a newspaper column. In creative writing, she has published ten poetry chapbooks and four full-length collections, over one hundred short stories, four novels, a novella, a short story collection and forty-one plays. As the Gilbert-Chappell Distinguished Poet she mentors student and adult poets. Her poem "Shaking Hands with Mountains" was previously published in Edgz, 1 (2001): 116-117. Garden Poems. Ed. Wanda Wade Mukherjee. Wake Forest, NC: The Scuppernong Press, 2005: 57-58. Mountain Writings: A Poetry and Prose Anthology. Ed. Tom Davis. Sylva, NC: Old Mountain Press, 2014: 29. The Mountain. Ed. Whitney Scott. Dyer, IN: Outrider Press, Inc., 2014: 100.
,
Mara Adamitz Scrupe is a poet and visual artist. She has exhibited nationally and internationally and has received numerous commissions, grants, fellowships and residencies. Scrupe's first chapbook *Sky Pilot* was nominated for the 2013 Library of Virginia Literary Awards. The National Federation of State Poetry Societies named Scrupe the winner of the 2014 Stevens Poetry Competition for her first book-length manuscript *Beast* slated for publication in June 2015. She is a professor at the University of the Arts in Philadelphia and divides her time between Philadelphia and Charlottesville, Virginia where she lives on a farm with her husband. Her poem "Now" will also appear in her book *Beast*.
,

Margaret Dubay Mikus, Ph.D. was a research scientist who healed from multiple sclerosis and cancer. Now a poet, singer and photographer, she is the author of three books of poetry. In 2013 she was the Illinois Featured Author for the Willow Review. Her poem "Watching Boats on the Lake" was previously published in her book *Thrown Again into the Frazzle Machine: Poems of Grace, Hope, and Healing.*

Marian Kaplun Shapiro was nominated for the Pushcart Prize in 2012. A Quaker and a psychologist specializing in the results of trauma, she is an unabashed peacenik. A five-time Senior Poet Laureate of Massachusetts, she is the author of a professional book and many related articles, one full-length poetry book and two chapbooks. Her poem "Vows" was previously published in *An Anthology Of Contemporary Love Poems* and her poem "Before (the) After" was previously published in the *Sufi Journal.*

Marilyn Peretti writes with poet colleagues in the western suburbs of Chicago. She has published the books *Let Wings Take You, To Remember-To Hope, Lichen-Poems of Nature,* and *Angel's Wings.* She has been published in *Talking River, Fox Cry Review, Christian Science Monitor, Journal of Modern Poetry, California Quarterly, www.poetrysky.com, Kyoto Journal* and others. Visit pagesbyperetti.com and perettipoems.wordpress.com.

Mary Jo Balistreri has published two books of poetry through Bellowing Ark Press and a chapbook through Tiger's Eye Press. She enjoys reading, long walks and gardening. Her poem "Boating on the Yerres" was previously published by Five Willows. Please visit her at maryjobalistreripoet.com.

Mary Langer Thompson's poetry appears in various journals and anthologies. She is a contributor to *The Working Poet* (Autumn Press) and *Women and Poetry: Tips on Writing, Teaching and Publishing by Successful Women Poets* (McFarland). She is a former school principal with an Ed.D. from the University of California, Los Angeles.

Nancy J. Heggem is a retired mathematician and former Trustee of the Palatine Public Library District. She is active with Northwest Cultural Council Poets and sponsors the annual poetry contest at the Palatine Public Library. Her work has been published in a number of Chicago area anthologies.

Peter Rodenby is a retired electrical engineer and full time grandfather who lives in an old cottage by a river with his wife. He has a degree in Earth Science and enjoys studying history and literature.

Richard King Perkins II is a state-sponsored advocate for residents in long-term care facilities. He is a three-time Pushcart nominee and a Best of the Net nominee and was a recent finalist in The Rash Awards as well as the *Sharkpack Alchemy, Writer's Digest* and *Bacopa Literary Review* poetry contests. His poem "Distillery of the Sun" was previously published in the *Bacopa Literary Review.*

Robin Lily Goldberg published her first poem at age six in *Spider Magazine*. After studying creative writing at Kenyon College and the University of Michigan, she published her first book of poetry, *Sound of Seeds*. When not writing, she teaches yoga and contributes to a storytelling program for hospital patients.

R.P.Muha says: "My only goal with publication is the realization of reaching a wider audience to convey the human experience we all share in life." Check him out at readingrpmuha.com.

S. M. Kozubek is an attorney, author and teacher. This is his third appearance in a *Journal of Modern Poetry* publication. He has also been published in *ICON*, *Frogpond*, *A Hundred Gourds*, *Prune Juice* and *bottle rockets*.

Susan Beall Summers has been published in numerous journals and anthologies including *Texas Poetry Calendar* and *Illya's Honey*. Visit her at tidalpoolpoet.com.

Susan Schaefer has worked in various fields—as a bookseller, hospital chaplain and as a CPA and financial consultant whose clients included a local publisher. Her children's book *Born to Shine* was published by her company, Blink Books. She currently volunteers at Open Books and writes poetry in her long-established writing group.

Tamara Tabel received a Silver Prize from Chicago Poetry Press for her poem "Albeit Macht Frei: Dachau 2012" which was subsequently selected to be included in *Poetica Magazine's* 2014 Holocaust Edition.

Thelma T. Reyna is a multiple national award-winning author and a Poet Laureate in Southern California. Her full-length collection of poetry *Rising, Falling, All of Us* has received national honors. Her new edited book of *60 poets Altadena Poetry Review: Anthology 2015* will be released in April 2015.

Tobin Fraley is the author of three books on the history of carousels, one children's book as well as the book *36 Acres*, a photographic and written exploration of the Reed-Turner Woodland Nature Preserve in Long Grove, Illinois. He is founder and director of the not-for-profit Long Grove Arts & Music Council (lgamc.org), member of the Barrington Writers Workshop, photography teacher at Chicago Botanic Gardens and a product designer. His poems and/or photography have been published in *Journal of Modern Poetry*, *Dark Matter* and *Gravel Literary Journal*.

Tracie Renee Amirante Padal's short stories and poems have won contests sponsored by *Scholastic*, *Seventeen*, *USA Weekend*, Xerox/DocuWorld, the Northwest Cultural Council, and Highland Park Poetry, and she has been published in *The Daily Herald*, *Bark*, *In Our Own Words: a Generation Defining Itself* and in the literary journals *Apocalypse*, *The Claremont Review*, *Louisville Review*, *Moon Journal*, and *Oyez Review*. She won first place in the nonresident category of the 2015 Highland Park Poetry Challenge. Tracie is a librarian and the proud mama of a son born with a heart defect (Transposition of the Great Arteries).

Made in the USA
Charleston, SC
29 March 2015